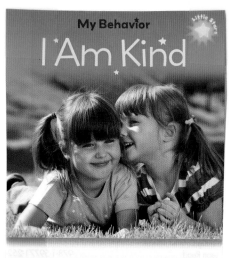

Titles

I Am Kind
Liz Lennon . . . . . .

I Can Help
Liz Lennon . . . . . .

I Don't Hit
Liz Lennon 978-1-59771-411-2

I Keep Clean
Liz Lennon 978-1-59771-412-9

Black Rabbit pg 3

Little Stars: My Behavi

This series of four books on being
helpful, polite, and clean does dou
by reinforcing good habits while
good reading practice. The vivid
controlled vocabulary, and lyrical
make these books fun to listen to ev
students are able to read themselves.

Sea-to-Sea Publications © 2013

Price
Individual Titles: $25.65 / **$17.95**
Complete Series of 4: $102.60 / **$71.80**

Reading Level: Grade K and up
Lexile level: available Fall 2012
Correlation with National Curriculum
NCSS 3, 4; CCSS 1, 2, 4, 5, 8

Specifications
Includes close photo-to-text match, carefully
controlled vocabulary, note to parents and
teachers
Graphics: Color photographs
Page Count: 24
Size: 6-5/8" × 6-5/8"

My Behavior
I Don't Hit

Liz Lennon

SEA-TO-SEA
Mankato Collingwood London

Sometimes I feel angry.

But I don't hit!

When Mom won't buy me candy, I feel angry.

But I don't hit!

Why?

Because hitting hurts and it makes people cry.

My friends left me out at playtime today.

It made me feel sad.

I said to my friends, "I want to play."

But I don't hit!

Sometimes my sister plays with my toys.

I wish my sister
would play with
her own toys.

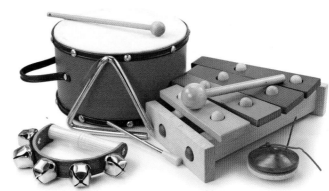

I feel really angry with my sister.

But I don't hit!

Sometimes I
just feel angry.

I don't
know why.

There's a knot inside my stomach that makes me feel like hitting out.

When I feel like this, sometimes it's best to be alone.

But other times I tell someone how I feel.

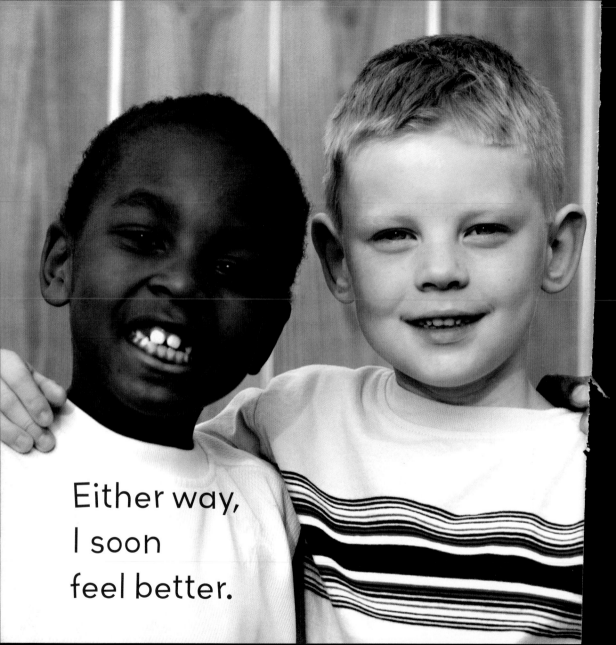

Either way,
I soon
feel better.

And I
never,
ever
hit!

About This Book

It is important for young children to learn that hitting is not acceptable, but some children find it hard to express their emotions in other ways. The aim of this book is to give you the opportunity to share and discuss different aspects of behavior and how it can be managed. Looking at and talking about the pictures is a good starting point.

Why we don't hit The main thing to get across is why we don't hit—because it hurts the person they hit. What would it feel like if someone hit us?

Feeling angry Discuss things that make the child angry, such as wanting something they can't have, having to share something of their own, or being left out. Why do they feel like this? What can they do instead? Tell them that their anger or frustration are normal feelings, but they have to express them with words only.

If they hit you If your child hits you, remain calm and make a sad face that shows you are hurt by their behavior. Tell them: "You hurt me! I'm sad you hit me. Hitting is not okay." Each unacceptable behavior must be taken seriously. If you don't act on it, you'll find it harder to take back control if your child develops a hitting habit.

If they hit other children Respond quickly and consistently. Never lose your temper. Model empathy by asking the other child if they are all right and apologizing on your child's behalf. Remove your child to create distance between the children. Acknowledge your child's feelings, and tell them firmly that hitting is not okay.

This edition first published in 2013 by Sea-to-Sea Publications

Distributed by
Black Rabbit Books
P.O. Box 3263, Mankato,
Minnesota 56002

Copyright © Sea-to-Sea Publications 2013

Printed in the United States of America, North Mankato, MN.

All rights reserved.

9 8 7 6 5 4 3 2

Published by arrangement with the Watts Publishing Group Ltd, London.

Library of Congress Cataloging-in-Publication Data

Lennon, Liz.
  I don't hit / written by Liz Lennon.
     p. cm. -- (Little stars : my behavior)
  Includes index.
  Summary: "Tells about different reasons a child gets angry and why it is important not to hit"--Provided by publisher.
  ISBN 978-1-59771-411-2 (alk. paper)
  1. Anger--Juvenile literature. 2. Violence--Juvenile literature. I. Title.
  BF575.A5L458 2013
  395.1'22--dc23
                                    2011052700

Series Editor: Sarah Peutrill
Art Director: Jonathan Hair
Series Designer: Paul Cherrill

Picture Researcher: Diana Morris
Consultants: Karina Philip and Deborah Cox

Picture credits: Fotolia: Godfer 2. Getty Images: Donna Day 12. Istockphoto: MShep2 18. Shutterstock: Blend Images 1, 21; Deepblue-Photographer 16r; Lane V Erickson 7; Gelpi 14, 15; Hartphotography 16l; Crystal Kirk front cover; Monticello 13br; Sergiy N 20; Ami Parikh 17b; Thomas M Perkins 23; Pixel Memoirs 6; Elena Schweitzer 13t, 13cl, 13cr, 13bl; Shebeko 5; John Steel 22; Tikona 17t. Superstock: Image Source 9, 11. Every attempt has been made to clear copyright. Should there be any inadvertent omission please apply to the publisher for rectification.

RD/6000006415/001
May 2012